Heart-Eyes Sometimes Hurt

Madison Taylor

Presentation by *BookLeaf Publishing*

Web: www.bookleafpub.com

E-mail: info@bookleafpub.com

ISBN: 978-93-95890-73-1

First edition 2022

DEDICATION

Cassius James

My Sun

Body of Gods

Rock

Murmur of swallows
Chitter little kites
One Pigeon flitters
To Distract the prey
Fungi of the dunes
Shriveled and woody
The quick of lizards
The spinafex grass
Tracks of a shy bird
In the underbrush
No magpies in sight
Hollers or chortles
Ghosts of centuries
Home in the centre

Uninhabited

Late winter blue sky
Warmest light Cool breeze
Here In the smack-bang
The furthest away
A Society
Monolith of rock
The brazen and brave
Where the sun is law
And the stars are gods

Thanking the heavens
Im leaving before
The season Changes
The spots on my face
Crows feet to my ears

Ill never forget
Desert oak and smiles
Truest of the time
Resilient man
The bearer of brunt
The hottest of suns
Calcify and task away
The mob that call shots
And Mob that belong
The souls old as time
Living on through new
Bodies living on
Spaces of their own
Heart home #1

Myth

Argos
        Hellebores
Born of tears. Sprout in snow.

'My daughters roam nude. Cursed madness
Save them'

Sands

Tin-Can Bay boat ramp
Tungsten glow through the sea-fret
Masts chime winds increase

The Curlew are leggy ladies
Near the end of the Rainbow
What the fuck's a Wobbegong?

Ground water She-Oak
Bush Turkeys will steal your food
Fishermans Dead-End

Tower

Youre my poison
I am your cure
Tainted in yellow
Violent and pure.

Happy moments
You caught to let go
Love me
Do you?
Forget me?
No.

Drain my river dry
Weeping willow
I am a tower
You are the sky.

Keep me in your songbook
All the other lovebirds
Defeated you twist
Spit me out

For in the end
Youre better without
Needing to be

Accountable

Capitalise
The pain you cause
Tell me Im wrong
I am a song

Beg for forgiveness
You confess
When I get the courage
To leave this mess

Pet

Another dead cat

One with road it lay apon

Beloved carcass

Power

Oh Wake
Open field
Cold clay Rotten leaves
Frozen in white where
The flowers are not.

Oh Here
Dew for days
Lowly the doe tracks
The red river gum
Perches on the bank.

Oh My
Moon glitters
On the stillest night
Hear the river sing
Echoes of the spur.

Oh Sweet
Dene and dale
The faint feather beat
White owl that sees all
but is seldom seen.

Hut

Piss rust

On the alloy basin

Tired window sheets

And a nest

Decorate the mantle

Warm light

From the sun room

Constellations of dust

And the landline Headset

Hanging onto home

Vessel

Knees bend
Dislocate
Snap and crumble
Knee is function

Knees don't joke
They do not lie
They demand attention
A literal support
For your upper portion

I am at war
With these knees
The mystery
My knees of Caution

On my knees
For these knees
Freedom is always
Just one step ahead

Hymn

The flowers
They bloom for you
Your eyes
Your nose
The sweet honey
The worker bees

To love
The endless journey
From flower to hive

Under the night sky
I gaze
And wonder

All that could
And is

The moon
Your soft lips
And the kisses you gift

With sounds
All around
I hear all

The blackbird hymn
And him
He sings
Like nothing else

Place

And there
On the cabinet
Above the kitchen bench

Angled light
Caught my eye

Revealing a series of forehead dents

Of all the idiots
Who banged their heads before him.

Holy

"The priest was a clown"

She prays

Smile

I like to see tall chimneys without a house.

Clouds in an otherwise cloudless sky, perched
around the mountain top.

I like to see hares lowering their ears to run
under the fence.

Steer leaning into a pole to scratch their behind.

Birds flying backward into the wind

Puddle

The waters flow

As water does

It was not unreasonable

To want the water to flow

But

In the beginning

I 'thought' so

I didnt see

It was a puddle

Full and muddied

Stagnant

A Time-being

Puddles displace

Evaporate

Bathed in by a bird

Polluted

Puddles rarely move

Or Improve

Sometimes council workers
Will fill them in.

I never wanted

A puddle

Balls

The words out

A young lady collecting seashells by the rock pools.

One by one
Old ladies with chests puffed.
Press about what's in my bag.

Only women
Have balls big enough to ask me what's in my bag.

The people walk by,
they scowl and speculate.

Each person gets the same answer and the same smile.

They all retreat
Defeated and deflated.

I'm collecting broken glass.

Everybody wants to know
but nobody wants to help.

Fire

Her new blossoms with vivid lightness
which cannot ever be diminished.

Softly, with grace.

Although her lands blackened.

Under heat and desire.

Judgement and shame.

The fire is a death and smoke is rebirth.

She never yearns for what was before the fire.

For her light only knows to grow,
No canopy to keep her hidden in the shade.

Stagnant energy, being fixed is no appeal.

Blooming, she is matchless she covers the land
with warmth and attention.

She is busy being, not appearing.

She is divine natural energy.

She flows.

She does not fight.

She has no apples of pears.
But she has some currants.

Hype

His hands of aggression

Gently they play

Twist and cure
Slice endure.

The generations of domination
Like his last and all before.

His fingertips
He presses.

Down around my throat
He needs.

My softness
My submission.

Im not hurt
Im not his victim.

He would detest
He knows best.

Correct my words
Reiterate my point.

He cant help himself
Leaning on the world.

But accuse
Others of using him.

Spring

It's that time of year.

The butterflies are fornicating and the flowers are new.

Shower

Anakie
not anarchy
'Yew yew'
The nightbird sang.

Sapphire blue
Cold in hand.

Fill the ashtray
Used for change.

The potaroo at pacey
Spooks a local.

Paul the prospector
with his dog named Tango

Dont want nothing. Dont got you.

Lawgy dawes has those howling dogs.

Lonesome creek to
Bears lagoon

Trailing back

Blink through
A little town called Banana

Got me fire got me food.

Everything I had
I gave it back
Dont want nothing
If I aint got you

Fuel

A Salix Babylonica live for the river bed break

Corymbia Cytriodora towers til' it dominates the
sky.

The Acacia Mearnsii are first to inhabit after
fire.

The empty 'Mountain Dew' bottle swollen in the
sun.
Fluorescent against the earthy landscape
Sticking out like dogs balls.

Red sand and plantain

Hot winds smell a way

The day long squint

Cotton mouth reminds I haven't seen water in a
while.

Just me and my JerryCan walking to collect
some petrol

Mute

I plead him to stop
It hurts when you talk to me that way
Instead
He stopped talking
Silence all day

His peaceful violence
So soft
He wouldnt physically
Hurt a fly
But his disapproving sigh
Could blow my brains

He speeds through the wet
Puts us at risk
Winding dark roads
I clench my jaw

I cannot watch
My eyes stay in my phone
If he kills me
I want it to be a suprise

Sun

I watch you when you sleep.
Your soft arms cradle your heart.
You lip little words.
And sometimes say "no" aloud
It fills me with pride.
To hear you assert yourself in your dreams.
You're milky glow is brightest in the moonlight.
The smell of you is the same as it was
The first time I held you.
And it feels the same holding you now.
As it did back then.
I stay up late sometimes.
Just to gaze in awe at you.

How did I get so damn lucky?

www.ingramcontent.com/pod-product-compliance
Lightning Source LLC
Chambersburg PA
CBHW060926130726
48001CB00006B/2437

A journey

ABOUT THE AUTHOR

Artist and Poet of over 20 years.
Madison first began her craft with Therapeutic intentions, leaning on the natural world and her lived experience.
She is an enthusiastic Bird Fancier, Prospector and Naturalist.
Madison is an Observer, Analytical, Intensely curious and loves a bit of satire which is evident throughout her practices.

CHLOE ROCHELLE

Borderline